Culver-Union Twp. Public Library
107 N. Main St.
Culver, IN 46511
574-842-2941/FAX 574-842-3441

Jobs People Do

Anita Ganeri

QEB Publishing, Inc.

Published in the United States by
QEB Publishing, Inc.
23062 La Cadena Drive
Laguna Hills, CA 92653
www.qeb-publishing.com

Library of Congress Control Number: 2005921248

ISBN 1-59566-076-3

Written by Anita Ganeri
Designed by Melissa Alaverdy
Editor Hannah Ray
Picture Researcher Nic Dean

Series Consultant Anne Faundez
Publisher Steve Evans
Creative Director Louise Morley
Editorial Manager Jean Coppendale

Printed and bound in China

Picture credits

Key: t = top, b = bottom, m = middle, l = left, r = right

Corbis/Ted Horowitz title page, 13t, / Paul A. Sauders 4b, /Adam Woolfitt 4t, 22mb, /Jim
Craigmyle 7, 18b, /Tom Stewart 8, 19t, /Jean Woodcock; Reflections Photo Library 11, 19b, /J.
Barry O'Rourke 12, /Reuters 13b, 20t, /Macduff Everton 14/Getty Images/Pornchai
Kittiwongsakul/AFP 5, / Taxi 10, 22b/NASA/16, 17, 21/Still Pictures/Jorgen Shytte 6, 22ml,
/Jose Lobao Tello 9t.

Contents

Farmer

Some farmers work on huge farms, like this one in New Zealand. The sheep farmer looks after thousands of sheep. He **shears** the sheep and sells their wool.

These farmers in Thailand have small
fields where they grow rice to eat.
They plant the rice in the ground.
The rice needs lots of water to grow.

Teacher

6

It is the beginning of the school day in Africa. The children say "Good morning" to their teacher. Then she takes the **roll**.

This teacher in Great Britain helps the children with their work. She listens to them read and helps them with their writing.

Vet

A vet is like a doctor, but he or she looks after animals instead of people.

If your pet is sick, you can take it to the vet and he or she will find out what is wrong.

8

Some vets look after wild animals in a wildlife park. The vets have to be careful because some animals can be very dangerous.

Nurse

Nurses work in a doctor's **clinic** or in a hospital. They usually wear uniforms, like these.

A nurse helps care for people when they are not feeling well.

10

Nurses have lots of jobs to do. They talk to the patients, bring them food, give them their **medicine**, and make their beds.

Firefighter

Honk! Honk! A fire engine is speeding along the street, with firefighters on board. The firefighters' job is to put out fires. It is dangerous, dirty work.

The firefighters use **hoses** to put out the flames. Sometimes, a fire spreads very far and fast. Then the firefighters may use planes to drop water onto the fire.

Mail carrier

How do letters and packages get to your house? You probably have a mail carrier who brings the mail every day. He or she may come on foot, or in a van or car.

But if you lived in a village in the desert in India, you would get a surprise. There, the mail arrives by camel!

15

Astronaut

16

Would you like to be an astronaut?

It's one of the most exciting jobs in the world. It takes years of hard work and training before you can blast off into space.

Astronauts often go for walks in space to do repairs on the space shuttle ... and they get an incredible view of planet Earth!

What do you think?

What do farmers in New Zealand do with the sheeps' wool?

Can you remember what the teacher is helping the children to do?

What does
a vet do when
you take your
pet to see him
or her?

A nurse does lots
of jobs. Can you
name some of them?

How can firefighters put out a fire that's spreading very fast?

Imagine you live in a desert village in India. How may your mail arrive?

Before you become
an astronaut, what
will you need to do?

Where does
an astronaut
go for a walk?
Can you
remember?

Glossary

Hoses—long pipes that squirt out water.

Medicine—tablets and injections to make people feel better.

Roll—a list of the names of the children in a class.

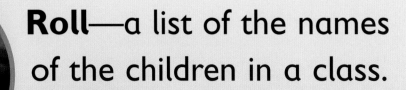

Shear—to cut off a sheep's wool with a special tool.

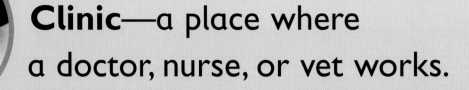

Clinic—a place where a doctor, nurse, or vet works.

22

Index

Parents' and teachers' notes

- Explain to your child that this book is nonfiction (i.e., that it provides facts and information, rather than tells a story). Point out that the book contains a contents page, a glossary, and an index.
- Explain that the reader can look at the contents page to see what the book is about. Explain that the contents page lists all the jobs that appear in the book, in the order in which they appear.
- Together, make a list of other jobs people do which could be shown in another book. Choose one of these jobs and write a page about it.
- Read pages 4–5 about farmers. Talk to your child about other things farmers grow and other animals they raise.
- Look at pages 6–7 about teachers. Encourage your child to talk about the kinds of things that his/her own teacher does, such as listening to him/her read.
- Talk to your child about taking a pet to the vet, or going on a trip to a wildife park. Has your child done either of these things? If so, encourage your child to describe his or her visit.

- Choose one of the jobs in the book and pretend that you do that job. Encourage your child to ask you questions about "your" job. Reverse roles and let your child imagine that he/she does one of the jobs featured in the book, while you ask the questions.
- Talk to your child about which job in the book he/she would most like to do. Why would your child like to do that particular job? Talk about the good and bad points about each of the different jobs.
- Leading on from pages 12–13 about firefighters, talk to your child about other people who work in the emergency services, such as police officers and paramedics. What types of things do these people have to do?
- Encourage your child to imagine what it is like to be an astronaut. Pretend to be astronauts on a space walk. Together, find out more about the training astronauts do, the equipment they use, and the clothes they wear. Help your child to create a fact sheet about astronauts. Can your child draw a picture to accompany your text?